111

THINGS TO DO

BEFORE YOU DIE

"Enjoy the little things in life, because one day you will look back, and realize they were the Big things."

Kurt Vonnegut

We never regret what we did, but we always regret what we didn´t.

We think we are going to live forever. But time is limited, and we procrastinate by leaving for tomorrow what we could be doing today.

These 111 things will help you live your life to the fullest

This is the perfect book to help you seize the day.

Don´t be like most people, which spend too much time dreaming instead of doing. You can either make plans now to do great things or let life pass you by.

You don't need to be rich to enjoy life. Most of the nicest things are for free.

Give yourself inspiration for what you can try next.

This is your personal guidebook to enjoying all that the world has to offer.

What are you going to do with the time that life gave you?

ENJOY THE SILENCE

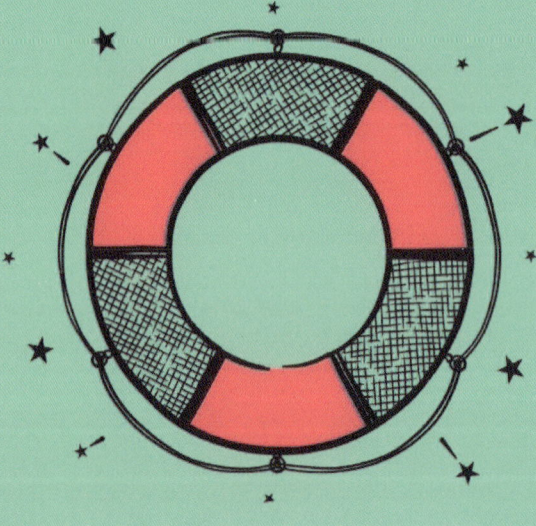

HELP SOMEONE

(even if you don´t know well that person)

WRITE A BOOK

(even if is just your travel journal)

CALL THAT SPECIAL PERSON

(to say I love you)

BE THE CAPTAIN OF YOUR LIFE

STUDY SOMETHING WEIRD

SAVE MONEY TO SPEND IN SOMETHING CRAZY UNFORGETTABLE

COMMIT TO SOMETHING

DESIGN YOUR LIFE

MAKE A MASTERPIECE

- Dance In The Pouring Rain
- Teach something
- Invite your neighbors over for coffee
- Dream awake
- Let Go Of Your Past
- Keep a dream diary
- Sleep 24hs
- Cover the bed in rose petals
- Camp out in the terrace
- Go mirrorless for a day

GO DIVING

MAKE A LIST OF THE THINGS THAT GIVES YOU GOOD VIBRATIONS

PLAY THAT OLD CASSETTE

TREAT RESPECTFULLY EVERYONE

GO TO WORK IN FLIP FLOPS

BUY YOURSELF FLOWERS

GET VITAMIN D, AT THE BEACH

TAKE A RIDE IN A HOT AIR BALLOON

INVENT YOUR OWN SMOOTHIE RECIPE

GET LOST

SPEND AN ENTIRE HOME CINEMA DAY

BALANCE YOUR BODY

LEARN TO PLAY GUITAR

SEND A MESSAGE IN A BOTTLE

- List the things your parents told you: one day you will understand…

- Watch the sunrise

- Go to the movies alone

- Run up an escalator the wrong way

- Go on a spontaneous road trip

- Learn how to appreciate being alone

- Bring a meal to a homeless person

- Get a Foot Massage

- Become comfortable speaking in public

- Write a cookbook

DANCE UNTIL YOUR FEET HURT

MAKE A BIG PARTY, FOR EACH BIRTHDAY

TAKE YOUR PASSPORT, GO TO AIRPORT AND TAKE THE FIRST AVAILABLE FLIGHT

PICNIC UNDER THE MOON

PLAY THAT OLD VIDEO GAME

MAKE PRESENTS

(even when there is no reason to do it)

PRINT YOUR PHOTOS

(don´t let them die in the PC)

PUT ALL THE PIECES OF YOUR LIFE TOGETHER

TAKE RISKS!

SAIL AWAY

LEARN TO SAY NO

SET A GOAL: ....

And reach it!

SETTLE DOWN

SPEND A WHOLE DAY SHOPPING

- Tie a sailors knot
- Do Everything With the Left Hand For a Whole Day
- Dress someone
- Visit a castle
- Blow Bubbles
- Recycle
- Be an expat once in your life
- do something big for charity
- relax

SING IN THE SHOWER

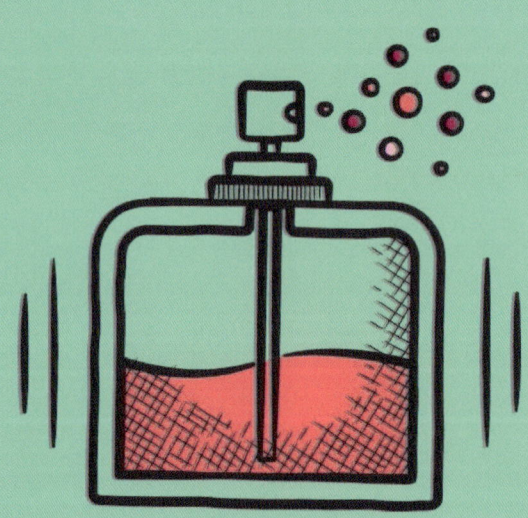

PERFUME YOUR BODY AND SLEEP NAKED

MAKE YOUR IDEAS COME TRUE

STARGAZE IN THE GRASS

SMILE!

Is the key to more open doors

INVEST WISELY YOUR TIME

PLANT A TREE

(at least a lemon seed)

TRAVEL LIGHT

HAVE A VISION

UNPLUG FROM DIGITAL WORLD

ATTEND A MUSIC FESTIVAL

HAVE A CLEANING DAY

(and get rid of things you don´t need anymore)

NO MORE SELFIES.

Instead enjoy more the moment

START UP SOMETHING

- Write a list of everything you're grateful for
- Research your family tree
- Learn to appreciate failure
- Witness the birth of a child
- Vacation solo
- Take a sabbatical from work
- Meditate
- Whatever you decide to do, just do it!
- Plant a community garden
- Vacation at a silent retreat
- Write a letter to your future self

RECORD VIDEOS WITH YOUR FAMILY

You will never regret of that

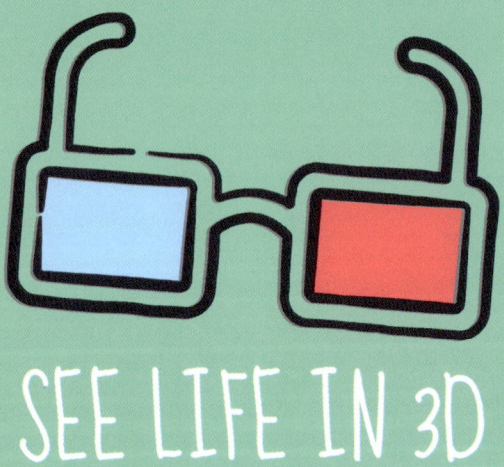

SEE LIFE IN 3D

(Slowly smelling, contemplating, tasting things)

REMEMBER WHO YOU ARE

FORGIVE

KEEP TRACK OF THE HIGHLIGHTS OF

YOUR DAYS

REMEMBER WHO IS

THE TREASURE OF YOUR LIFE

EAT HEALTHY

GO ON HOLIDAYS
WITH YOUR BEST FRIEND

- Adopt a furry friend
- Stop trying to change people
- Find your first love
- Kiss a stranger
- Send someone an anonymous gift
- Share a fantasy
- Wake up 30 minutes earlier than usual
- Give Blood
- Invent a new trend
- Make a dream board
- Be yourself

ADD YOURS:

-
-
-
-
-
-
-
-
-
-

Copyright © 2016
By BARCELOVER®

Designed in Barcelona

All rights reserved
This book or any portion thereof
may not be reproduced or used in any manner whatsoever
without the express written permission of the publisher
except for the use of brief quotations in a book review
Illustrations by Shutterstock / Denk Creative

Printed in Great Britain
by Amazon